T0209460

An Analysis of

Chris Argyris's

The Individual and Organization: Some Problems of Mutual Adjustment

Stoyan Stoyanov

Published by Macat International Ltd
24:13 Coda Centre, 189 Munster Road, London SW6 6AW.

Distributed exclusively by Routledge
2 Park Square, Milton Park, Abingdon, Oxon OX14 4RN
711 Third Avenue, New York, NY 10017, USA

Routledge is an imprint of the Taylor & Francis Group, an informa business

www.macat.com
info@macat.com

Cataloguing in Publication Data
A catalogue record for this book is available from the British Library.
Library of Congress Cataloguing-in-Publication Data is available upon request.
Cover illustration: A. Richard Allen

ISBN 978-1-912303-97-7 (hardback)
ISBN 978-1-912284-68-9 (paperback)
ISBN 978-1-912284-82-5 (e-book)

Notice
The information in this book is designed to orientate readers of the work under analysis,
to elucidate and contextualise its key ideas and themes, and to aid in the development
of critical thinking skills. It is not meant to be used, nor should it be used, as a
substitute for original thinking or in place of original writing or research. References and
notes are provided for informational purposes and their presence does not constitute
endorsement of the information or opinions therein. This book is presented solely for
educational purposes. It is sold on the understanding that the publisher is not engaged
to provide any scholarly advice. The publisher has made every effort to ensure that
this book is accurate and up-to-date, but makes no warranties or representations with
regard to the completeness or reliability of the information it contains. The information
and the opinions provided herein are not guaranteed or warranted to produce particular
results and may not be suitable for students of every ability. The publisher shall not be
liable for any loss, damage or disruption arising from any errors or omissions, or from
the use of this book, including, but not limited to, special, incidental, consequential or
other damages caused, or alleged to have been caused, directly or indirectly, by the
information contained within.

CONTENTS

THE MACAT LIBRARY

The Macat Library is a series of unique academic explorations of seminal works in the humanities and social sciences – books and papers that have had a significant and widely recognised impact on their disciplines. It has been created to serve as much more than just a summary of what lies between the covers of a great book. It illuminates and explores the influences on, ideas of, and impact of that book. Our goal is to offer a learning resource that encourages critical thinking and fosters a better, deeper understanding of important ideas.

Each publication is divided into three Sections: Influences, Ideas, and Impact. Each Section has four Modules. These explore every important facet of the work, and the responses to it.

This Section-Module structure makes a Macat Library book easy to use, but it has another important feature. Because each Macat book is written to the same format, it is possible (and encouraged!) to cross-reference multiple Macat books along the same lines of inquiry or research. This allows the reader to open up interesting interdisciplinary pathways.

To further aid your reading, lists of glossary terms and people mentioned are included at the end of this book (these are indicated by an asterisk [*] throughout) – as well as a list of works cited.

Macat has worked with the University of Cambridge to identify the elements of critical thinking and understand the ways in which six different skills combine to enable effective thinking.
Three allow us to fully understand a problem; three more give us the tools to solve it. Together, these six skills make up the **PACIER** model of critical thinking. They are:

ANALYSIS – understanding how an argument is built
EVALUATION – exploring the strengths and weaknesses of an argument
INTERPRETATION – understanding issues of meaning

CREATIVE THINKING – coming up with new ideas and fresh connections
PROBLEM-SOLVING – producing strong solutions
REASONING – creating strong arguments

To find out more, visit **WWW.MACAT.COM.**

CRITICAL THINKING AND "THE INDIVIDUAL AND ORGANIZATION: SOME PROBLEMS OF MUTUAL ADJUSTMENT"

Primary critical thinking skill: REASONING
Secondary critical thinking skill: PROBLEM-SOLVING

The impact of "The Individual and Organization: Some Problems of Mutual Adjustment" depends heavily on reasoning skills. Chris Argyris uses strong, well-structured arguments to make his point. He presents the individual as an integral part of the work process and understands that the work process also forms an important part of the individual's development. Argyris establishes that managers expect individuals to work toward achieving the organization's objectives. However, he also observes a lack of reciprocal engagement from managers to recognize and satisfy the development needs of employees. This reasoning convinces the reader of the validity of Argyris's demand that managers deliver prospects for the employee's development and stimulate the transition from childhood to adulthood.

Argyris's reasoning has strong implications for solving a problem that many organizations experience: disengaged and disloyal employees. He proposes that satisfying the development needs of employees is likely to result in higher loyalty to the organization and greater commitment to its goals. Individuals who are managed according to his principles are therefore expected to exercise higher self-control and be more efficient.

ABOUT THE AUTHOR OF THE ORIGINAL WORK

Chris Argyris (1923–2013) was an influential management theorist and a pioneer in organization development. He was Professor of Education and Organizational Behavior at both Harvard Graduate School of Education and Harvard Business School. He earlier helped create the Yale School of Management. His work on how organizations learn and the relationships between people and organizations is considered seminal. Argyris was acclaimed as an exceptional teacher. In addition to his research and teaching, he worked as a consultant. "The Individual and Organization: Some Problems of Mutual Adjustment" was published in 1957.

ABOUT THE AUTHOR OF THE ANALYSIS

Stoyan Stoyanov holds a PhD in Management from the University of Edinburgh. His research focuses on overcoming difficulties in internationalization. Dr. Stoyanov's other research interests include reducing liabilities of outsidership of individuals; newness, smallness, and foreignness of organizations; and the ways in which individuals embed themselves in new local environments.

ABOUT MACAT

GREAT WORKS FOR CRITICAL THINKING

Macat is focused on making the ideas of the world's great thinkers accessible and comprehensible to everybody, everywhere, in ways that promote the development of enhanced critical thinking skills.

It works with leading academics from the world's top universities to produce new analyses that focus on the ideas and the impact of the most influential works ever written across a wide variety of academic disciplines. Each of the works that sit at the heart of its growing library is an enduring example of great thinking. But by setting them in context – and looking at the influences that shaped their authors, as well as the responses they provoked – Macat encourages readers to look at these classics and game-changers with fresh eyes. Readers learn to think, engage and challenge their ideas, rather than simply accepting them.

'Macat offers an amazing first-of-its-kind tool for interdisciplinary learning and research. Its focus on works that transformed their disciplines and its rigorous approach, drawing on the world's leading experts and educational institutions, opens up a world-class education to anyone.'

Andreas Schleicher
Director for Education and Skills, Organisation for Economic
Co-operation and Development

'Macat is taking on some of the major challenges in university education ... They have drawn together a strong team of active academics who are producing teaching materials that are novel in the breadth of their approach.'

Prof Lord Broers,
former Vice-Chancellor of the University of Cambridge

'The Macat vision is exceptionally exciting. It focuses upon new modes of learning which analyse and explain seminal texts which have profoundly influenced world thinking and so social and economic development. It promotes the kind of critical thinking which is essential for any society and economy. This is the learning of the future.'

Rt Hon Charles Clarke, former UK Secretary of State for Education

'The Macat analyses provide immediate access to the critical conversation surrounding the books that have shaped their respective discipline, which will make them an invaluable resource to all of those, students and teachers, working in the field.'

Professor William Tronzo, University of California at San Diego

WAYS IN TO THE TEXT

KEY POINTS

- Chris Argyris was a management theorist and pioneer in organization development who worked at Harvard Business School.

- Argyris's article scrutinizes the impacts that management, strict organizational configurations, and control mechanisms have on individuals.

- He provides insight into how organizations can adapt to individuals and their needs to make the most out of their symbiotic relationship.

Who Was Chris Argyris?

Chris Argyris (1923–2013) was the son of Greek immigrants and grew up in Irvington, New Jersey and Athens, Greece. During World War II,* he joined the US Army Signal Corps,* eventually reaching the rank of Second Lieutenant. Argyris graduated with a BA in Psychology from Clark University in 1947. He later went on to gain an MA in Psychology and Economics from Kansas University in 1949 and a PhD, under the supervision of William Whyte,* from Cornell University in 1951.

Argyris is an influential American management theorist and a pioneer in organization development. In a career that spanned more than 50 years, he played a formative role in the development of our understanding of individuals, organizations, learning, and change. He was Professor of Education and Organizational Behavior at both Harvard Graduate School of Education and Harvard Business School. He also worked as a professor at Yale University for 20 years and helped create the Yale School of Management.

Argyris was the first to seriously argue that conventional management practices create a fundamental conflict between organizations and people. He also argued that this conflict is inherently harmful to both because organizations treat employees like children. Argyris's passion for management science sets him apart from many other scholars in his discipline. All his work focused on furthering this area of knowledge, which made him a respected and often-cited authority in this field.

Argyris put his research into practice by using his position as a member of the Organization Development Professional Guild to investigate how new ideas worked—or did not work—in real business environments. As a result, and unlike most university scholars, he became equally influential in academia and business.

Argyris realized that although organizations may be absorbed by production and profit goals, they pay far less attention to the best ways of achieving them. He therefore argued for fundamental change. He wanted to see ineffective working practices replaced by new processes that take into proper account the needs of both individuals and organizations, thereby creating a more sustainable future for both.

Argyris spent a lifetime researching, teaching, consulting, and advocating. His article "The Individual and Organization: Some Problems of Mutual Adjustment," published in 1957, issued a wake-up call to three key groups: individuals, managers, and academics. The central principles he outlined on how organizations should develop are recognized as practical and useful, and the significance of his findings have only increased over time. We live in a world that is increasingly dependent on large formal organizations and many of us work for them. Therefore, Argyris's work will remain relevant for generations to come.

What Does "The Individual and Organization: Some Problems of Mutual Adjustment" Say?

In "The Individual and Organization," Chris Argyris argued that organizations should be flatter. Flatter organizational systems* facilitate information exchange between individuals and groups at all levels. The efficient flow of information from the top down and from the bottom up characterizes a flat organizational structure. Such an organizational structure, Argyris proposes, also enriches the information that it channels. This is because it includes what is often omitted: the opinions and experiences of individuals within the organization. Collecting and circulating all ideas, rather than privileging those that conform to existing ideas and policy, improves decision making and allows organizations to capitalize fully on employee expertise.

Argyris also argued for the implementation of a leadership structure that encourages open dialogue between managers and their teams. He suggests that such a structure allows for better communication. It also boosts information processing and tactical planning capabilities, emphasizes joint objectives, and allows all employees to feel part of the decision-making process. The author's belief in the value of flat management systems can be traced back to his wartime experience in the US Army Signal Corps. That the efficiency of any network can be improved by better communication is an insight that underpins almost all his work.

"The Individual and Organization" did more than recognize that businesses are often badly run and that existing structures make poor use of employee capabilities. It also makes the case for remodeling the system on several levels simultaneously. Argyris wrote for employees, managers, and academics, thus pressing his case in different sectors and at different levels. As a consequence, his analysis of the relationships between organizations and individuals generated interest among social scientists (e.g. Peter Senge).* It also provided managers with insights on how to retain organizational pride and increase productivity sustainably. At the employee level, Argyris urged individuals to be proactive even if their formal job descriptions did not demand it.

Among the most important of Argyris's insights was the effectiveness of addressing all three of these groups simultaneously. While each group might take its own steps to implement change independent of the others, joint efforts would significantly increase overall awareness and solutions. Just as importantly, Argyris recognized that each of the three groups must respond to changes actioned by the other two. For example, business academics notice and study the changes that take place in organizations, while managers cannot ignore employee demands for personal and professional development. Argyris believed that even if only one group responded to his argument, it would be sufficient to catalyze change. Finally, it should be noted that Argyris expected his argument to have a greater impact on individuals than on the other two groups. He equated the move from being passive to being active with the progression from infancy to adulthood.

Why Does "The Individual and Organization: Some Problems of Mutual Adjustment" Matter?

"The Individual and Organization" was ahead of its time in its understanding of capitalist* and industrial labor relations, making its lessons completely relevant today. It draws much of its power from the author's educational background in psychology, economics, and organizational behavior.* This background allowed Argyris to take account of existing approaches to behavioral science and human motivation. He used them not only to understand the sources of disharmony between individuals and organizations, but also how to overcome them. Argyris's determination to help managers implement necessary change led him to incorporate ideas from several different academic disciplines, including sociology, psychology, and anthropology. He blended these ideas into what was ultimately a hugely original contribution to the field of management.

Argyris's core ideas derive from his direct observations of a time of substantial change in business organizations in the early twentieth century. Significantly, Argyris witnessed the creation of corporate structures in the United States. This period saw substantial urbanization and the concentration of the labor force in organizations. This was a change analogous in character, if not in scope, to the Industrial Revolution.* Changes in managerial practice and the way organizations were evolving compelled Argyris to look for new theories and enrich existing ones in response to the problems that these changes raised.

Argyris saw human beings as individuals with complex needs and suggested that satisfying those needs would produce both psychological well-being and higher productivity in the workplace. His analysis of complex needs helped managers understand how individuals think about the work process and the workplace environment. Argyris insisted that improving the interaction between individuals and organizations benefits both.

Argyris's work has inspired debate among social scientists on the relationship between formal organizations and individuals. It significantly improved understanding of organizational learning* and organizational action* in ways that influenced both individuals and the whole discipline of management science. Thanks to his contribution, the themes of organizational learning and organizational action have enriched organizational studies.*

MODULE 1
THE AUTHOR AND THE HISTORICAL CONTEXT

KEY POINTS

- Argyris's focus on individual attitudes and behavior is in line with the thinking of Mary Parker Follett,* Elton Mayo,* Abraham Maslow,* and Douglas McGregor.*

- The fast-growing corporate structures at the time of publication served as an encouraging context for developments in scientific management.

- According to Argyris, the creation of adjustment strategies* could improve the relationship between individuals and organizations.

Why Read This Text?

Chris Argyris has influenced generations of business leaders, fellow scholars, and students. His paper, "The Individual and Organization: Some Problems of Mutual Adjustment," was published in 1957 at an early stage in his long career. It alerts the reader to the core issues of behavioral science research on organizations. Individuals and organizations are juxtaposed and the incompatibility between the two is indicated, or at least implied, by the title of the article. Argyris did indeed conceptualize this relationship as lacking in harmony and requiring change. The title of the article arouses interest in why and how the social entity—the organization—is inharmonious with its composite parts—the individuals.

Argyris did not prioritize either individuals or organizations in his analysis and this symmetry draws attention to the relationship between the entities. The implementation of strategies to improve this

> ❝ Ideally, healthy development in our culture involves growth from being passive as an infant to being active as an adult; from being dependent to being relatively independent; from being in a subordinate position to achieving equal or higher position than friends achieve; from expressing few and shallow abilities to expressing many and deeper abilities. ❞
>
> Chris Argyris, "The Individual and Organization"

relationship requires analysis from different standpoints. Argyris analyzes the need for individuals to value themselves and aspire to an increased sense of competence. He also examines how organizations can help employees define goals, create paths to achievement, evaluate their effectiveness, and increase the challenge of work. This dual analysis seeks to prescribe ways in which both employees and companies can function more effectively.

Author's Life

Chris Argyris stands out among management theorists. He was like a psychotherapist in the way he evaluated complex organizations* and placed them within a systematic framework of relationships. Argyris's formidable educational background—BA in Psychology (Clark University, 1947), MA in Psychology and Economics (University of Kansas, 1949), and PhD in Organizational Behavior (Cornell University, 1951)—gave him the cross-disciplinary intellectual breadth to enrich the field of behavioral science. He did so by focusing on workplace relationships and addressing the sources of tension between individuals and organizations.

Argyris joined Yale University in 1951, serving as the Beach Professor of Administrative Sciences and as chair of the Administrative Sciences Department. He was instrumental in the creation of the Yale

School of Management. In 1971, he moved to Harvard University and was appointed the James Bryant Conant Professor of Education and Organizational Behavior.

Argyris further tested and refined his theoretical approach at the Research Center for Group Dynamics (established at the Massachusetts Institute of Technology* and relocated to the University of Michigan). There he was significantly influenced by the Center's founder, Kurt Lewin,* a seminal social psychologist. Lewin theorized on group dynamics, leadership styles, experiential learning,* and the importance of understanding the individual in his or her social context.

Argyris became a major figure in the behavioral school of management.* This school focuses on human relations and employee well-being, and encourages management approaches that assume employees are motivated to work. Argyris's focus on individual attitudes and behavior is consistent with the works of other major behavioral theorists such as Mary Parker Follett, Elton Mayo, Abraham Maslow, and Douglas McGregor.

The behavioral school can be contrasted with the classical school of management which dates to the Industrial Revolution. This school, based on classical organization theory,* focuses on improving efficiency, productivity, and output. It does not focus on behavioral attributes or variances among employees, such as how job satisfaction can improve efficiency.

Author's Background

The start of the twentieth century was a period of rapid change in organization theory which included the synthesis of management, administrative, and bureaucratic theories. Scientific management theory,* which aimed to increase labor productivity by analyzing and manipulating workflows based on earlier ideas of economic efficiency, was in vogue by the 1910s. It aimed to match individuals to the tasks they can do best. Motivational forces were limited to supervision, rewards, and penalties.

Planning and control were the preoccupations of the period, but their effectiveness when applied to more complex organizations was in doubt. Effective planning and control for complex organizations came later, when Argyris revolutionized the field.

Argyris's sociological approach in "The Individual and Organization" built on other notable twentieth century works including Lillian Gilbreth's* *Psychology of Management* (1914) and Peter Drucker's* *Concept of the Corporation* (1946). The limitations of existing theories motivated Argyris to send a clear message to both theorists and managers who want to enhance their competitive advantage through increased productivity.

Argyris believed that the widely accepted pyramidal scheme* of top-down management style was the source of much mistrust within organizations. Argyris answered the need of business owners and managers to increase productivity through sustainable means, rather

ACADEMIC CONTEXT

KEY POINTS

- Chris Argyris diverged from the traditional Theory X,* which is based on a concept first articulated by Sigmund Freud.*

- The lack of balance between Theories X and Y* led to the development of Theory Z* by Abraham Maslow.

- Accommodating the complexity of human nature allowed Argyris to reach more nuanced conclusions in his thinking than in Theories X and Y.

The Work In Its Context

Chris Argyris's work on the relationship between organizations and individuals transcended contradictions between earlier theories. It is worth briefly examining these earlier approaches, known respectively as Theory X and Theory Y. These theories represent two sets of assumptions about human nature and behavior that are relevant to the practice of management and have different practical implications for the workplace.

Theory X was first put forward by the famous founder of psychoanalysis,* Sigmund Freud. It essentially posits that people are idle, avoid responsibility, and will only work to gain security through monetary payment. It also suggests that people are best motivated by the coercion of using rewards and punishments. This dim view of human nature downplays the potential positive role of individual initiative and trust within an organization. It sees a repressive work environment as conducive to better productivity.

In contrast to this, management professor Douglas McGregor articulated Theory Y in the early 1960s. Theory Y suggests that

> **❝** [That] formal organization can be altered by personalities ... is not denied by formal organizational experts. **❞**
>
> Chris Argyris, "The Individual and Organization"

individuals go to work of their own accord because work is the only way they can satisfy their needs for achievement and self-respect. It assumes that most people generally enjoy work and responsibility, and will be committed to their organization if the work is satisfying and rewarding.

Theory Y is an expression of the humanistic school of thought* in management. It sees people as primarily motivated by their own beliefs and desires (intrinsic motivation)* rather than by external influences or rewards (extrinsic motivation).* An individual's desire to learn and develop is regarded as a leading motivational force upon which managers can capitalize. However, Theory Y gives management no easy excuses for failure. It challenges them to innovate and discover new ways of organizing.

Overview of the Field

The oppositional nature of Theories X and Y had been synthesized through Theory Z, put forward by psychologist Abraham Maslow. Maslow was a contemporary of Freud and a scholar on the individual's pursuit of self-actualization. Maslow developed a theory of motivation based on human needs. More specifically, he suggests that individuals are motivated by their unsatisfied needs.[1] The individual's aspiration to fulfill desires and develop strengths through interesting, challenging tasks is widely acknowledged to be a powerful behavioral agent.[2] Theory Z represents a humanistic approach to management. Proponents of Theory Z suggest that common cultural values should promote greater commitment among employees to the organization.

Argyris built on all these schools of thought. According to him, organizational management must be reshaped, as the old pyramidal structure had proved unable to fully utilize individuals' capabilities and energy.[3] Flatter hierarchical structures encourage individual initiative, self-motivation, and development. The betterment of organizations would naturally follow from individual empowerment.

Though Argyris's humanistic approach was not in itself original, the originality and merit of his specific theories are recognized by the behavioral school of management. Therefore, it is not surprising that Argyris has generated intellectual debate among theorists and social scientists on the relationship between organizations and individuals. The result has been a better understanding of organizational learning and organizational action.

Academic Influences

The originality of Chris Argyris's work "The Individual and Organization: Some Problems of Mutual Adjustment" remains undisputed by social scientists. Argyris focused on industrial organizations and evaluated their management practices as well as the consequences these practices have for individuals. Through micro-level analysis* of experiential learning, he investigated how a top-down management approach, in which decision-making is retained at the top management level, affects behaviors within organizations. This approach is a particularly original way of exploring ingrained problems in organizations and serves as a great contribution to performance-oriented research.*

Incorporating individual behavior into his theoretical framework allowed Argyris to reach beyond the contradictions of Theories X and Y. In an interview with Robert M. Fulmer* in 1998, Argyris reaffirmed that the motivation for his work had been to help managers.[4] His work was practical and targeted at real-life problems in the workplace. This is significant because organizations have become a fundamental part of the individual's maturation process. For many people, their career and development objectives are realized through work in an organization. The continuation of this relationship between individuals and organizations assures the relevance of Argyris's work for generations to come.

NOTES

1   Abraham H. Maslow, *The Farther Reaches of Human Nature* (New York: Viking Press, 1971).

2   Abraham H. Maslow, "A theory of human motivation," *Psychological Review* 50 (1943): 360–96.

3   Chris Argyris, "The Individual and Organization: Some Problems of Mutual Adjustment," *Administrative Science Quarterly* 2 (1957): 1–24.

4   Robert M. Fulmer and Bernard J. Keys, "A conversation with Chris Argyris: The father of organizational learning," *Organizational Dynamics* 27(2) (1998): 21–32.

THE PROBLEM

KEY POINTS

- Chris Argyris challenged fundamental principles of how organizations should be managed.

- It remains unclear how formal organizational structures and individuals interact, and whether their interaction changes formal structure.

- Mary Parker Follett proposed that integrating the views and needs of managers with those of the workforce facilitates conflict identification and resolution.

Core Question

While examining the relationship between organizations and individuals in "The Individual and Organization: Some Problems of Mutual Adjustment," Chris Argyris challenged the fundamental principles of how organizations should be managed. To improve organizational structures, he undertook a comprehensive investigation of organizational and human behaviors. As such, his work is designed to answer a range of questions, including:

- What are the properties and characteristics of a formal organization?
- Do formal organizations have any impact on human personality?
- How do organizations influence individuals and how do they respond?
- How can educated individuals become more active in pursuing the success of the organization?

> **❝** If formal organization is defined by the use of such principles as task specialization, unity of direction, chain of command, and span of control, then employees work in a situation in which they tend to be dependent, subordinate, and passive to a leader. **❞**
>
> Chris Argyris, "The Individual and Organization"

In his analysis, Argyris brought organizations and individuals closer together and observed the reactions of individuals placed under a tightly controlled organizational model.

Answering the above questions is crucial for revealing problems of mutual adjustment that might occur behind the scenes. Moreover, the answers allow a better understanding of individuals and organizations separately, before bringing them together to scrutinize the viability and functionality of their bonds. The use of adjustment strategies to increase unity between individuals and organizations requires that their relationships be examined from different standpoints. Argyris's approach to the above questions uses these perspectives.

The Participants

When "The Individual and Organization" was published in 1957, the major intellectual battle in management theory was between proponents of Theories X and Y. Theory X assumes that individuals are lazy, need to be controlled, and will not work without monetary incentives. The theory rejects the importance of self-initiative and trust in the workplace, and regards an authoritarian work atmosphere as essential for productivity and efficiency. Argyris's reasoning diverged from this view.

Theory Y assumes that people are naturally motivated by intrinsic, as opposed to extrinsic, incentives. A person's aspiration to learn and improve is regarded as the principal motivational force, and the manager's job is to unite the labor force.

Argyris stood apart from the mainstream by offering a bilateral analysis that considered both organizations and individuals. He suggested that structures influence individuals as much as individuals affect formal structures.

Ultimately, Argyris addressed the core questions relatively broadly. A partial explanation for this could be that his assumptions about organizations and personality are taken to extremes in the text to emphasize the results. Another explanation is the author's ambition to sketch an open framework that could be used for further analysis of individuals and organizations. The framework described in "The Individual and Organization" is intended to stimulate management scientists to theorize about the mutual impacts of each on the other.

The Contemporary Debate

Argyris's ideas were influenced and shaped by the work of Australian-born psychologist Elton Mayo.[1] In the first half of the twentieth century, Mayo dismissed the idea that individual motivation and job fulfillment could be achieved solely through monetary incentives. His theories on additional sources of motivation, however, were not extensively circulated during his life. Only later was he recognized as having laid the foundation for the human relations strand of management science.

Mary Parker Follett, a contemporary of Freud, was another prominent thinker and management consultant whose views on organizational theory and behavior foreshadowed those of Argyris. She proposed that integrating the views and needs of managers with those of the workforce was the only certain way to identify and resolve workplace conflict.[2] Other methods of conflict resolution, such as force or compromise, were not only ineffective, but damaging to both sides. This idea is generally consistent with Douglas McGregor's Theory Y.[3]

Argyris expanded the work of the above scholars and contributed significantly to the behavioral management field. He used insights from his predecessors and contemporaries to produce uniformity in the new behavioral school of management. Argyris shook the foundations of the classical school of thought by crediting increased productivity to worker motivation and satisfaction.

NOTES

1   Mayo, E., *The Human Problems of an Industrial Civilization* (London: Routledge, 2014).

2   Follett, M.P., *The New State: Group Organization the Solution of Popular Government* (University Park: Penn State Press, 1918).

3   Douglas McGregor, *The Human Side of Enterprise* (New York: McGraw-Hill Professional, 2006).

THE AUTHOR'S CONTRIBUTION

KEY POINTS

- Chris Argyris clearly showed the discrepancies between individual expectations and formal organizational structures.

- Argyris's view that the organizational system needs to be adapted is supported by another major theme in his text: human nature.

- Argyris addressed the issue of change in the workplace by suggesting that a satisfied workforce can deliver enhanced performance.

Author's Aims

"The Individual and Organization: Some Problems of Mutual Adjustment" clearly indicates Chris Argyris's orientation toward the humanistic values of Theory Y. His work challenges the pyramidal value system which underpins Theory X. It rejects the view that employees are normally lacking ambition and are reluctant to take responsibility.

Argyris argued that, for most organizations, the collective was more important than the individual. As a result, employees were denied agency and were unable to act as change-makers within an organization. Most formal organizations, he said, fit individuals to the job like tools, rather than allowing them to adapt their work environment to fit their unique capabilities. Argyris provided evidence for this by drawing attention to concepts such as task specialization,* chain of command,* and span of control.* These concepts focus on building organizational and *administrative* efficiency rather than *production* efficiency. The two aims were out of sync.

> ❝ It is the purpose of this paper to outline the beginnings of a systematic framework by which to analyze the nature of the relationship between formal organization and individuals. ❞
>
> Chris Argyris, "The Individual and Organization"

Argyris also identified the discrepancies between individual expectations and formal organizational structures. His work suggests that satisfying the developmental needs of employees would be beneficial for both entities. Establishing a balance between the needs of both individuals and organizations would provide a sustainable source of increased productivity and a competitive advantage.

Approach

Argyris makes clear in the introduction of "The Individual and Organization" that his examination of organizational behavior is intended to be a starting point for further academic research and is primarily targeted at the United States and some Western European cultures.

Argyris systematically demonstrates the lack of balance between formal organizations and employees. He argues that monetary incentive, as management's only means of responding to discontent, is not a sustainable way of resolving conflicts between individuals and formal structures.

Argyris focused on control as an inadequate management tool. Specifically, he examined how organizations not only perceive control as necessary, but use it too much. This overemphasis inevitably leads to a workforce that is passive, apathetic, dissatisfied, and reluctant to take responsibility. This path is hard to reverse and easily results in inefficiencies and loss of personnel.

Argyris considered the role of human nature in his search for ways to address workplace discord. He believed that, as people grow and develop, the maturation process is accompanied by the emergence of new needs and demands. For example, with maturation comes the desire for more independence, the expansion of interests and activities, and the development of longer-term goals. Organizations that exert very tight control impede a worker's innate developmental needs and potential. Such organizations, in effect, treat individuals like children.[1]

Contribution in Context

The core concepts presented in Argyris's "The Individual and Organization" originate from his observations of a period of rapid change. Between 1880 and the late 1920s, industrialization and urbanization expanded in the United States faster than ever before. The country attained urban-majority status between 1910 and 1920. This time of rapid urbanization saw further industrialization of the workforce. This meant that manufacturing in factory settings used machines and a labor force with unique, divided tasks to increase production. It was during this period of change that the relevance of Theory X, which suggests that only financial incentives can lead to efficiency, was challenged.

Argyris derived insights from both Theory X and Theory Y as he developed his vision. According to him, the management of organizations had to be redesigned because the traditional pyramidal structure is unable to utilize individual capabilities and energy. A flatter and less hierarchical structure would significantly advance the personal and professional progress of workers, and self-motivation would become widespread. Productivity would grow and organizational reputation would be enhanced.

For the first time in management science research, individual human characteristics were central to the analysis. This intellectual departure, in which Argyris was a central figure, said that increased organization performance in a period of rapid social change could only be built upon a satisfied workforce. This new behavioral management theory aimed to amplify managerial incentives for improving work conditions, believing that the greater the employees' satisfaction, the higher the productivity.

NOTES

1   Chris Argyris, "The Individual and Organization: Some Problems of Mutual Adjustment," *Administrative Science Quarterly* 2 (1957): 1–24.

SECTION 2
IDEAS

MAIN IDEAS

KEY POINTS

- Chris Argyris asserted that establishing trusting relationships within organizations results in greater efficiency and effectiveness.

- By rejecting the belief that greater control leads to better productivity, Argyris's work belongs with the humanistic value camp.*

- Argyris generated dialogue between academics and practitioners about the relationship between formal organizations and individuals.

Key Themes

Chris Argyris was an advocate of Theory Y and asserted that establishing trusting relationships within organizations would result in greater efficiency and effectiveness. This would also motivate individuals to develop their potential and better contribute to the attainment of the organization's overall goals.

"The Individual and Organization" presented a direct challenge to the pyramidal scheme of classical theorists. It rejected the rather misanthropic belief that people are by default idle, unmotivated, without ambition, and unwilling to assume responsibility in the workplace. By highlighting the psychological changes and developmental phases that come with the transition from childhood to adulthood, Argyris proved that treating adults like children is a counterproductive business practice. Tight control of workers by managers, which was a core element of the pyramidal value system and a common industrial practice, relegated individuals back to the

> ❝ Since in real life the formal structure and the individuals are continuously interacting and transacting, it seems useful to consider a study of their simultaneous impact upon each other. ❞
>
> Chris Argyris, "The Individual and Organization"

state of a powerless childhood. This denial of a worker's innate developmental needs naturally resulted in alienation and tension in the workplace.[1]

Argyris's immaturity-to-maturity theory gained wide academic acceptance. Beyond academia, business managers also heeded his advice. His proposed understanding of behavioral management has since dominated over the ideas of the pyramidal value system. At present, Argyris's stance that pyramidal values lead to mistrustful relationships which hinder efficacy is commonly accepted. The established dominance of the humanistic value system created momentum for the development of the behavioral management field, for which Argyris's immaturity-to-maturity theory provides a foundation.[2]

Exploring the Ideas

By rejecting the conventional notion that higher control produces better productivity, Argyris's work fits into the humanistic value camp. He also claimed that pyramidal or hierarchical organizational structures lead to superficial and fragile relationships between workers and organizations. Such structures hinder the natural expression of ideas so that workers are unable to enrich their own organizations.

By building on the work of others such as Mary Parker Follett, Elton Mayo, Abraham Maslow and Douglas McGregor, Argyris shaped a seminal work that has withstood criticisms from classical organizational theorists. The classical school is now weak and its core ideas have been overturned (e.g. the notion that individuals are motivated only through control or monetary incentives). For scholars, the classical school is now mainly of historical and comparative interest.[3]

Of course, this does not mean that all organizations are now run according to a more democratic and humanistic value system. Many fall well short of a management system that nurtures individual development and leads to intra-organizational balance. Argyris did not provide a definitive blueprint for organizations to follow, so managers are left to their personal and often conflicting interpretations. The gap between theory and practice remains.

"The Individual and Organization" is nonetheless regarded as a great and original contribution to behavioral management science.

Language and Expression

Argyris investigated the relationship between organizations and employees, and rejected the existing consensus on how organizations should be managed for optimal performance. He realized that improving organizational structures required the comprehensive exploration of their two central entities: organizational behavior and human behavior. Consequently, Argyris designed his work around posing and answering a range of questions, including:

- What are the properties and characteristics of a formal organization?
- Do they impact human personality in any way?
- How do organizations influence individuals and how do individuals respond?

Exploring these questions is critical for illuminating the dynamics between formal organizations and individuals. It enables a better understanding of each entity individually before studying the sustainability and functionality of their relationships with each other.

There is a discrepancy between what individuals need and expect, and what formal organizations demand and provide. This lack of balance can lead to frustration, insecurity, conflict, short-term orientation, and organizational failure.

The way Argyris expressed his theories and findings makes it unsurprising that he has generated intellectual dialogue among academics and practitioners about the relationships between organizations and individuals. His goal was to foster further research on how individuals could obtain optimum expression and how organizations could obtain optimum satisfaction of their demands at the same time.

NOTES

1   Magnus Ramage and Karen Schipp, *Systems Thinkers* (London: Springer, 2009), 279-283.

2   Jill Anderson, "Remembering Professor Chris Argyris," *Harvard Graduate School of Education News and Events*, November 22, 2013, accessed January 22, 2018, https://www.gse.harvard.edu/news/13/11/remembering-professor-chris-argyris.

3   Mary Jo Hatch and Ann L. Cunliffe, *Organization Theory* (Oxford: Oxford University Press), 145.

MODULE 6
SECONDARY IDEAS

KEY POINTS

- Chris Argyris's vision influenced subsequent research into organizational theory.

- Argyris argued that flatter organizational structures would facilitate data exchange to all levels of the organization.

- Argyris suggested innovative managerial practices to encourage the optimum satisfaction of both individuals and organizations.

Other Ideas

Some secondary themes in "The Individual and Organization: Some Problems of Mutual Adjustment" assumed a central role in Chris Argyris's subsequent work. Their significance is indicated through their influence on a range of social scientists across various disciplines.

The secondary ideas relate to the consequences of a lack of harmony between formal organizations and mature individuals. What distinguishes them from the core concepts is their focus on individual behaviors and actions.

According to Argyris, individuals will adapt to basic organizational failures. Adaptations may take the form of any of the following: acculturating, attempting a promotion, defensiveness, aggression, apathy, decreased productivity, cheating, or quitting the job.

These subordinate ideas fulfill the author's aspiration to increase the influence and scope of behavioral management studies. The themes are integral to the dilemma of how managers will meet individual needs and organizational demands in a sustainable way that goes against neither human nature nor organizational goals. The

> ❝ How is it possible to create an organization in which the individuals may obtain optimum expression and, simultaneously, in which the organization itself may obtain optimum satisfaction of its demands? Here lies a fertile field for future research in organizational behavior. ❞
>
> Chris Argyris, "The Individual and Organization"

solution lies in building an organization that enables individual freedom of expression without sacrificing organizational goals. By discussing the subordinate ideas without fully testing them, Argyris paves the way for other scholars to engage in the field of behavioral management.

Exploring the Ideas

Chris Argyris advocated the establishment of a flatter organizational system that facilitates information exchange up and down all levels of an organization, regardless of individual positions or seniorities. This is characteristic of less hierarchical formal structures. He argued that including the input of all employees would enrich the scope and quality of information upon which company decisions are based. This would also help achieve a more sustainable coexistence.

Argyris thereby seemed to advocate shared leadership. This relies on open communication and facilitates shared objectives. The author's belief in this management system can be traced back to his own experience. His affiliation with the US Army Signal Corps taught him the importance of communication in the efficiency of a network. This understanding is obvious in his work; he suggests that better communication means greater information processing and tactical planning capabilities within an organization.

"The Individual and Organization" was a major contribution to the evolution of organizational behavior and employee relations theories. Its critique of specialization, the chain of command, and financial rewards have fostered great dialogue since its publication. Argyris's conclusion that organizations should respond to differences in human nature and adjust their structures and policies to meet individual needs was groundbreaking.

Overlooked

One major aspect of the text which is of potential significance for organization and management theory appears to have been overlooked. Although the academic community has followed most of the research directions Argyris suggested, his followers have not developed a specific managerial practice for realizing both individual and organizational satisfaction. Although Argyris called this research strand "a fertile field for future research in organizational behavior," it remains unclear how it can be achieved in practice.[1] This is mainly because of the various forms of organizations that were conceptualized and the different types of personalities within them. Even so, the author suggested the establishment of communities within organizations in which managers and employees are regarded as equal. He posits this as a feasible way of bridging the interests of organizations and individuals.

Argyris said that the solution lies in enhancing the independence of employees in the workplace. Flattening hierarchies and emphasizing democratic leadership has been found to increase creativity, but greater worker autonomy might also mean that employees become less focused on the objectives of the organization. Democratic decision-making has a cost for any organization.

Argyris provided a theoretical solution to the conflict between the worker's need to be treated as a mature individual and the organization's need to do so with caution. However, the practical application of the theory is challenging. Argyris left the articulation of new managerial practices to future scholars of organization and management science.

NOTES

1   Argyris, C., 1957. The individual and organization: Some problems of mutual adjustment. *Administrative science quarterly*, 1.

MODULE 7
ACHIEVEMENT

KEY POINTS

- Chris Argyris was successful at shifting focus away from the organization-centered classical theory to a person-centered approach.

- Argyris promoted the remodeling of organizational management so that it fully utilizes the capabilities and energies of individuals.

- His work is still relevant as many organizations still adhere to the pyramidal system.

Assessing the Argument

Evaluating the current relevance of Chris Argyris's paper, "The Individual and Organization: Some Problems of Mutual Adjustment," is best done within the school of thought from which it sprang. Its usefulness may be gauged by considering two opposing value systems: the pyramidal value system and the humanistic value system.

Argyris advocated the latter and asserted that establishing trusting relationships within organizations results in greater efficiency and effectiveness. The humanistic system provides individuals with motivation to develop their potential and better contribute to the attainment of organizational goals.

This understanding of behavioral management science soon became dominant. Argyris's argument that pyramidal values create mistrustful relationships and hinder efficacy is commonly accepted today. Given this general shift from the organization-centered classical theory to a person-centered approach, Argyris's efforts should be deemed successful. The wide approval he received from the

> **❝** Bringing together the evidence regarding the impact of formal organizational principles upon the individual, we must conclude that there are some basic incongruences between the growth trends of a healthy personality in our culture and the requirements of formal organization. **❞**
>
> Chris Argyris, "The Individual and Organization"

organizational management community can be illustrated with the work of Marlena Fiol.* Fiol stated that the process of improving organizational actions should be achieved through better "knowledge and understanding."[1] Mark Dodgson* is more precise when he notes that organizational efficiency should be achieved by better utilizing the broad skills of the workforce.

Achievement in Context

In industrial society, organizations are the principal context in which individuals realize their development aims. The rapid spread of industrial organizations in the early twentieth century was the context for the emergence of Argyris's psychological management concepts based on the individual.

"The Individual and Organization" has influenced not only academic research, but also management practice and society more broadly. Wider public knowledge of the article is a consequence of Argyris's skill as a teacher and communicator. Throughout his career, he was a teacher, consultant, and researcher. As a member of a professional guild, he crossed freely from management research to management practice and was equally influential in both worlds.

"The Individual and Organization" was a wake-up call to three groups: employees, managers, and academics. It increased awareness that organizational management needed to be remodeled, as existing structures did not fully utilize the capabilities of individuals. The paper's simultaneous reach to these three groups achieved multilevel change. Argyris did more than generate intellectual debate among social scientists. He went beyond academia to reach managers and provide them with insight on how to regain organizational pride and increase productivity in a sustainable way.

Limitations

The person-centered approach remains relevant and applicable today, as many companies would benefit from being run in a less hierarchical manner.

However, Argyris has his critics. His theory remains highly experimental and descriptive. The deductive nature of his contribution was regarded as a potential limitation even by the author himself, until later revisionists reinforced the theory by combining behavioral and quantitative tools. This is often done by surveying large samples of people and tracking similarities in their behavior. This synthesis was intended to enhance the theory's logic and reasoning, as well as to extend its applicability to different organizational contexts. Overall, the critics' response to this additional work, which developed the questions originally posed by Argyris, has been positive. For an example, see Delbert C. Miller's* "*Integrating the Individual and the Organization: Chris Argyris.*"[2]

The cultural relevance of the work is another consideration. Argyris's findings are based on ideal or extreme examples of individuals and organizations. This does not always fit other cultural contexts. For example, in environments where people do not have such a strong desire to be mature, or in organizations where the overarching culture does not make people dependent and passive, the article's impact could be challenged. This may invite criticism as to the theory's relevance.

NOTES

1   Fiol, C.M. and Lyles, M.A., 1985. Organizational learning. *Academy of management review*, 10(4), 803.

2   Delbert C. Miller, *"Integrating the Individual and the Organization: Chris Argyris,"* American Journal of Sociology 71, no. 1 (1965): 108-109.

PLACE IN THE AUTHOR'S WORK

KEY POINTS

- Chris Argyris's "The Individual and Organization: Some Problems of Mutual Adjustment" laid a solid foundation for a very successful academic career.

- The consistency of his work suggests that Argyris was a mature thinker even at the initial stages of his professional development.

- "The Individual and Organization" is regarded as a great contribution to behavioral management science.

Positioning

Chris Argyris's "The Individual and Organization: Some Problems of Mutual Adjustment" was published as a short article in 1957. Despite being one of the first works in his impressive output, it was far from tentative or underdeveloped. It laid a solid foundation for a very successful academic career. Although his subsequent books provided deeper analyses and confirmed his contributions to the behavioral school of management, it is important to recognize the value "The Individual and Organization" brought to his reputation.

By devoting himself to understanding organizational norms and group dynamics, Argyris established his position as a prominent behavioral scientist. An original contribution from among his subsequent works can be found in the article "Single-Loop and Double-Loop Models in Research on Decision Making," published in 1976.[1]

This article noted that the potential of learning and feedback in the organizational decision-making process was largely ignored. The

> ❝ This dilemma between individual needs and organization demands is a basic, continual problem posing an eternal challenge to the leader. ❞
>
> Chris Argyris, "The Individual and Organization"

commonly used single-loop learning* did not incorporate feedback. In single-loop learning, people or organizations modify their actions if outcomes are not what was expected. They follow rules and modify actions to get a different result. Argyris articulated a double-loop learning* model for providing feedback and more effective decision-making. With double-loop learning, people or organizations do not only modify actions; they also look at whether the underlying causes, or operating assumptions, need to be changed. The decision-making rules are therefore changed.

This and other subsequent work built on "The Individual and Organization." They all consider individuals, personalities, and behaviors alongside organizations. Argyris remained particularly focused on the challenge of making the relationships between individuals and organizations mutually beneficial, compatible, and harmonized.

Integration

The evident consistency throughout Argyris's work suggests he was a mature thinker even at the initial stages of his professional development. Throughout his career, Argyris expressed the notion that individuals are intrinsically motivated. He argued that this provides opportunities for greater mutual benefit if organizations are willing to create a fruitful environment for individuals to reach their full potential. This understanding surfaced in Argyris's early work and persisted throughout his career. His consistency in exploring the practical problems which stem from a pyramidal management structure strongly indicates the importance he attached to these issues.

Argyris challenged the ways in which organizations are managed. His principles on how organizational structures can be improved are widely acknowledged and regarded as highly practical. They are also likely to remain relevant for years to come, as his works continue to be cited. Argyris is the father of organizational learning, and his publications demonstrate his deep interest in improving conditions for both employees and managers. He founded a research center within Harvard University and was one of the directors of a high-profile consultancy firm in Cambridge, Massachusetts called the Monitor.

Significance

"The Individual and Organization" was influenced by a time of rapid evolution in industrialization and organizational theory in the early twentieth century. Detailed planning and organizational control were fundamental concepts of that period, but their value in the operation of organizations eventually came to be disputed. Behavioral approaches to planning and management were later introduced by Argyris. He noticed the limitations of conventional practice and revolutionized the field with his humanistic approach.

Argyris attempted to achieve the generalization and replicability that support a successful theory. Therefore, "The Individual and Organization" possessed undisputed practicality as organizations started to play an important role in the maturation of individual workers.

"The Individual and Organization" is regarded as a great contribution to behavioral management science and a core work in the field of organizational learning. Argyris laid the foundations of the field by exploring entrenched organizational problems from an original perspective. This has been regarded as influential to performance-oriented research.

It is therefore unsurprising that this short article spurred so much intellectual debate on the dynamics between organizations and individuals. The outcome has been an improved understanding of organizational structure, organizational learning, and how to resolve problems between individuals and organizations.

NOTES

1 Argyris, C. (1976), "Single-Loop and Double-Loop Models in Research on Decision Making", *Administrative Science Quarterly*, Vol. 21, No. 3, 363-375.

SECTION 3
IMPACT

MODULE 9
THE FIRST RESPONSES

KEY POINTS

- Chris Argyris's work was initially vigorously challenged. This is perhaps due to disagreements between the classical and humanistic schools of thought, and the author's orientation toward the latter.

- Argyris was explicit in describing human beings as individuals with complex needs.

- Argyris insisted that his work was not single-dimensional (i.e. focused exclusively on the employees and not the organization).

Criticism

The main themes of Chris Argyris's "The Individual and Organization: Some Problems of Mutual Adjustment" were initially vigorously challenged by his contemporaries. Management science at the time was characterized by a split between two opposing schools of thought: classical and humanistic. Argyris had a strong orientation toward humanistic values and took a behavioral approach.

The challenge Argyris presented to the classical, pyramidal value system lead to scrutiny by classicists in return. Argyris's psychological focus on the personal maturation process, the drive for self-actualization, and the analogy with human evolution was deemed insufficient to fully explain organizational change processes. Peter Senge was one such critic. He articulated the concept of learning organizations* in addition to the learning individuals* implied in Argyris's work. For Senge, learning individuals are only one aspect of organizational learning.[1] His framework includes the need for team

> **❝** It can be shown that job enlargement and employee centered ... leadership are elements which, if used correctly, can go a long way toward ameliorating the situation. **❞**
>
> Chris Argyris, "The Individual and Organization"

learning, shared vision, managers' learning, and strategy adaptation capabilities.* These additional dimensions are seen by some as essential in understanding organizational learning and change.

In the book *Integrating the Individual and the Organization* (1972), Argyris acknowledged that helping organizations transform into self-learning organizations was a more challenging task than he had earlier imagined. The author stated the following: "I did not realize the degree to which human beings, in many different cultures, have been programmed through socialization to deal with embarrassment or threat in ways that are counterproductive to their own intentions."[2] He called this skilled incompetence,* and argued that it results in organizations being limited systems.[3]

Responses

In subsequent works, Argyris responded to criticisms of his analytical focus on the individual.[4] He denied that his work was single-dimensional and focused only on employees. He made it explicit that he saw human beings as individuals with complex needs. He argued that organizations are a product of how employees regard and represent the organizational structure. He said that organizations are organisms comprised of multiple actors and that organizational learning stems from these actors. In other words, organizations tend to be static, but individual agency and development form the cognitive capacities of organizations. However, organizations are also reflexive, which allows the organizational learning stemming from individuals to permeate throughout.

Argyris also developed the idea of double-loop learning in response to his critics. He thought that single-loop learning only delays problem-solving. Double-loop learning, with its feedback mechanism, led to real change in how organizations solve and prevent problems. Argyris claimed that organizational change stems from individual needs and that this is sustainable in the context of double-loop learning. His analysis of organizational learning and its influence on the development, productivity, and flexibility of organizations was a convincing response to those who questioned the practicality of his work.

Conflict and Consensus

Because Argyris did not provide concrete examples in "The Individual and Organization," its practical application for organizational management was challenged immediately upon publication. Argyris took this criticism seriously and affirmed in a much later interview that his intention had been to produce actionable knowledge.[5] His subsequent work explained the multidimensional nature of his ideas more fully. Even toward the end of his life, Argyris continued to work to improve methods of learning.

Argyris's model is not as multidimensional as others and is based on extreme or ideal types. For example, individual needs and organizational demands are characterized simply with organizations acting as the suppressors of individual developmental aspirations. In addition, Argyris acknowledged in his subsequent work *Integrating the Individual and the Organization* that he did not thoroughly explore what caused organizations to produce pyramidal structures in the first place. It could be argued that the pyramidal organizational structure was developed precisely because employers and managers paid attention to the important features of human beings. This statement helps to reach the consensus that one should study the organizational design of a particular company before determining whether the pyramidal structure is inhibiting or facilitating the work process.

Even so, it is generally accepted that "The Individual and Organization" lay the groundwork for the betterment of organizational structures. The article also provided the basis for Argyris's other publications in communication and training practices. His entire body of work is integral to the development of behavioral management science.

NOTES

1   Peter Senge, *The Fifth Discipline: The art and practice of the learning organization* (London: Random House, 1990).

2   Chris Argyris, *Integrating the Individual and the Organization* (New York: Routledge, 2017): 1.

3   Chris Argyris, *Integrating the Individual and the Organization* (New York: Routledge, 2017): 1.

4   1) Chris Argyris, "The individual and organization: An empirical test," *Administrative Science Quarterly* 4 (1959): 146–67; 2) Chris Argyris, "Creating effective research relationships in an organization," *Human Organization* 17 (1958): 34–40; 3) Chris Argyris, "The organization: What makes it healthy?" Harvard Business Review 36 (1958): 107–16; 4) Chris Argyris, "Management implications of recent social science research," *Personnel Administration* 21 (1958): 5–10.

5   Robert M. Fulmer and Bernard J. Keys, "A conversation with Chris Argyris: The father of organizational learning," *Organizational Dynamics* 27(2) (1998): 21–32.

MODULE 10
THE EVOLVING DEBATE

KEY POINTS

- The idea of enhancing organizations by acknowledging individual needs became pervasive in all layers of management.
- Enhancing communication within organizations stimulates new knowledge and ideas.
- Modern management schools of thought accept that formal organizations are complex entities.

Uses and Problems

"The Individual and Organization: Some Problems of Mutual Adjustment" is a landmark work in the behavioral school of thought. It explores the relationship between the individual and the organization and provides a new understanding of imbalances between them. It has had a growing influence on generations of scholars and has provided a conceptual foundation for modern management practice.

Scholars such as Donald Schön* and Robert Putnam* have reinforced Chris Argyris's finding that intense control and demand for submission are poor management practices. Mark Dodgson supports that view by suggesting that a successful organization requires managers to "improve the use of broad skills of their workforces."[1] In the decade following the article's publication in 1957, academics started to regard good leadership as the ability to establish a beneficial relationship rather than to control. Argyris's humanistic legacy soon became conventional wisdom and is now an accepted way of managing complex organizations.

> **❝** Is there a way out of this circular process? The basic problem is the reduction in the degree of dependency, subordination, submissiveness, and so on experienced by the employee in his work situation. **❞**
>
> Chris Argyris, "The Individual and Organization"

The idea of enhancing organizational operations by considering individual maturation needs became pervasive across management theory and practice. Addressing these needs improves worker output, superior–subordinate relations, and multilevel communications within companies. Improved relationships and communications help motivate long-term workplace learning, creativity, and contributions.

Schools of Thought

Argyris's idea of organizational learning eventually fueled intellectual debate across the scholarly community. The goal of achieving organizational learning through improved communication reached another level of theoretical abstraction through Niklas Luhman.* Luhman was a German social theorist who saw organizations as collections of communications, not collections of individuals. This theoretical construct fortified Argyris's insistence on the importance of open communication for organizational learning and evolution to take place.

Later authors such as psychologist Edgar Schein* have observed that organizations learn slowly and have difficulty modifying traditional organizational practices. As a result, organizations operating in dynamic contexts cannot maneuver swiftly to benefit fully from their business environment. For example, they cannot adopt new practices quickly even if they see them being successfully utilized by a competitor. Although the study of this dilemma emerged in more recent years, it flows from Argyris's original contribution.

An extension of Argyris's ideas is that learning in organizations is a result of the communication of individuals. Consequently, if an organization is to adjust to a fast-changing environment, its embedded communication patterns must change. Enhancing communication across all levels of the organization will stimulate the emergence of new knowledge that will allow quicker and smoother organizational adaptations during turbulent times.

Argyris's ideas have continually been reinforced and extended by the academic community. Examples are "Organizational Culture and Leadership" by Edgar Schein and "The Knowledge-Creating Company" by organizational theorists Ikujiro Nonaka* and Hirotaka Takeuchi.*[2] This has shaped Argyris's work as a seminal piece that has contributed to the growth of several generations of scholars and at least two schools of thought: humanistic and management.

In Current Scholarship

"The Individual and Organization" contributes to the understanding of the inharmonious relationship between individuals and organizations. Argyris advanced behavioral management science and continues to inspire research. His measureable impact meant not only the further development and application of his ideas, but also the modernization of management science itself.

The modern management school of thought accepts that formal organizations are complex entities. Complexity encompasses both organizational structure and the diverse needs, objectives, motives, and aptitudes of individuals. This demonstrates Argyris's view that individuals play a role in organizational change.

Critics such as sociologist Delbert C. Miller argued that Argyris placed insufficient emphasis on collective learning within organizations. This alleged lack of multidimensionality was addressed by Argyris's followers. Researchers such as Senge adopted Argyris's focus on individual needs in the learning process, but also included the need for team learning, shared vision, managers' learning, and strategy adaptation capabilities.[3] These additional variables strengthen Argyris's work and allow research on professional behavior within organizations to be more systematic and practical.

Argyris's ideas were taken up by many revisionists in the modern school of thought who combined input from different academic streams. The deductive nature of Argyris's contribution can be regarded as a potential limitation, but his work has been reinforced by the rich empirical research that followed to test his ideas. The resulting combination of Argyris's original work and later scholarship has facilitated a completeness of logic and reasoning, as well as a wider applicability to a broad range of organizational situations.

NOTES

1   M. Dodgson, "Organizational Learning: A Review of Some Literatures." *Organizational Studies* 14(3): 375.

2   1) Schein, E.H., *Organizational Culture and Leadership* (Hoboken: John Wiley & Sons, 1985). 2) Nonaka, I. and Takeuchi, H., 1995. *The Knowledge-Creating Company: How Japanese Companies Create the Dynamics of Innovation* (Oxford: Oxford University Press, 1995).

3   Peter Senge, *The Fifth Discipline.*

IMPACT AND INFLUENCE TODAY

KEY POINTS

- Chris Argyris's immaturity/maturity theory has gained prominence and managers have started to take his advice into consideration.

- Highlighting the interplay between organizations and the individual's maturation process has significantly contributed to management theory and practice.

- Following Argyris's work, contemporary research tries to translate academic findings to organizational practices.

Position

Chris Argyris postulated that management must provide opportunities for the employee's development in order to make the individual an integral part of the work process and engage them in the organization's objectives. This was likened to the transition from childhood to adulthood. It moved from passivity to activity, from dependence to independence, from simple behavior to complex behavior, from superficial to profound interests, from short-term to longer-term perspective, from a subordinate position to an equal position, and lastly, from a lack of self-awareness to full self-awareness.

Argyris's immaturity/maturity theory has gained wide acceptance among academic theorists. In the business world, managers have also started to take his advice into consideration. Moreover, numerous consulting companies specializing in productivity enhancement have adopted Argyris's vision as the driving force for their strategies. The utility of the immaturity/maturity theory is therefore apparent today.

> ❝ Employees tend to work in an environment where (1) they are provided minimal control ... (2) they are expected to be passive (3) they are expected to have a short-time perspective, (4) they are induced to ... value the frequent use of a few superficial abilities, and (5) they are expected to produce under conditions leading to psychological failure. ❞
>
> Chris Argyris, "The Individual and Organization"

Although he advocated humanistic practices in the workplace, Argyris did not articulate a precise blueprint for companies or consultants to follow. Different organizations have found different strategies and have had to experiment to find the best path toward the organizational gains Argyris outlined. This in part explains why many organizations still appear static in their development even though their managers appear determined to obtain the organizational gains outlined by Argyris. Such organizations can experiment with the company's governance system to identify which practices nurture individual development, create balance, and lead to multilateral gains.

Interaction

"The Individual and Organization: Some Problems of Mutual Adjustment" (1957) was published at a time when humanistic principles in management science were not the standard. Argyris developed a new, systematic framework to study behaviors within complex, multidimensional organizations. His analysis of the interplay and contradictions between the demands of formal organizations and the maturation aspirations of individuals resulted in a powerful contribution to the organizational management school of thought. His ideas are now embedded in management science.

This can be shown by the change in how scholars view and define "learning." Chris Argyris and Donald Schön defined organizational learning as "the detection and correction of error."[1] Later, Marlena Fiol defined learning as "the process of improving actions through better knowledge and understanding."[2] Mark Dodgson explains organizational learning as "the way firms build, supplement, and organize knowledge ... and develop organizational efficiency by improving the use of broad skills of their workforces."[3] George P. Huber* suggests that learning occurs in an organization "if through its processing of information, the range of [the organization's] potential behaviors is changed."[4]

It is unsurprising that Argyris generated intellectual dialogue among both academics and practitioners on the relationship between organizations and individuals. He employed insights from his predecessors and contemporaries to establish a new wave of behavioral management. He shook the foundations of the classical school of thought with powerful works that regarded worker motivation and satisfaction as the engine of productivity. His work gained wide acceptance among other notable scholars who built upon it in their own research, such as Donald Schön, Robert Putnam, and Diana McLain Smith.*

The Continuing Debate

The ideas in "The Individual and Organization" are not part of current intellectual debates with opposing schools of thought. The article is accepted as a seminal work and, as such, its validity is rarely disputed. Moreover, the school of thought to which it belongs remains a historical point of reference.

The paper retains its value by having created a context for research that has lasted to the present day. An ideal result for contemporary research is for academic findings to translate applicably to practitioners.

In the case of Argyris, this ideal has only been partly realized, as many formal organizations have not succeeded in adopting his propositions.

The concept of learning organizations has remained popular due to the desire of organizations to be more agile and adaptable to change. The learning of individuals and organizations can facilitate the growth of the company and its ability to adapt over time. Adaptation and change are inevitable in a competitive and shifting market. Learning, as presented by Argyris, is a dynamic concept. To utilize its assets, organizations need to adopt flexible structures and dynamic processes that enable organizational learning and promote experimentation.

Attempts to translate Argyris's academic findings into practice have not only provided fertile ground for new research in management science, but have also created a wealth of opportunity for consulting companies.

NOTES

1   C. Argyris, and D. Schön. *Organizational learning: A theory of action perspective* (Reading, Mass: Addison Wesley), 12.

2   C. M. Fiol, and M.A. Lyles. "Organizational Learning." *Academy of Management Review* 10(4): 803.

3   M. Dodgson, "Organizational Learning: A Review of Some Literatures." *Organizational Studies* 14(3): 375.

4   G.P. Huber. "Organizational learning: The contributing processes and the literatures." *Organization Science* 2(1): 88-115.

MODULE 12
WHERE NEXT?

KEY POINTS

- Focus remains on how organizations could be developed by balancing their needs with those of individuals.

- Chris Argyris initiated enduring debates among social scientists on the relationships between organizations and individuals.

- Argyris's ideas and contributions will remain pertinent in the future.

Potential

The power of "The Individual and Organization: Some Problems of Mutual Adjustment" is evident in the original thought of the author, Chris Argyris, who built upon existing organization theory. Argyris's work is also well-placed in the context of industrialization and the rise of formal organizations in the United States at the beginning of the twentieth century. At this time, formal organizations became the predominant context for the realization of individual development aims. The relevance to this context, as well as its generalization and replicability, allowed "The Individual and Organization" to introduce a well-established theory that fit the peculiarities of the time. In addition, the work possesses practicality regarding the potential for organizations to enable the maturation of workers.

The central concepts Argyris identified responded to the question of how organizations could develop while balancing their needs with those of individuals. The relevance of these concepts and their influence on academic discourse continues today. Argyris's core messages, including the immaturity/maturity theory, continue to be

> **❝** This analysis is part of a larger project whose objectives are to integrate by the use of a systematic framework much of the existing behavioral-science research related to organization. **❞**
>
> Chris Argyris, "The Individual and Organization"

sound as social relations become ever more complex. Complex formal organizations are still a fact of life, as is the lack of mutual adjustment between organizations and individuals. Individuals still have a role in realizing mutual adjustment in a very complex environment. Though "The Individual and Organization" is the product of a simpler age, it still has much to offer today.

Future Directions

The originality of Argyris's work remains largely undisputed by social scientists. It focuses on the context of industrial organizations, the evaluation of management practices, and the impacts and consequences for individuals. The micro-level analysis examines the influence and cost of a top-down decision-making approach. This is a particularly original way of exploring embedded organizational problems and serves as great contribution to performance-oriented research.

Due to the largely appealing insights of his work, Argyris easily spawned intellectual discussions among the scholarly community. Theorists and social scientists focused on the relationship between organizations and individuals, and are likely to continue to do so in the future.

Argyris was a vocal advocate of job enrichment. He continually suggested that companies need to emphasize hiring a whole person, not merely a pair of hands. In his more than 30 books, he reiterated the benefits for organizations when they encourage individuals to reach their full potential. Argyris believed that people already possess inherent energy and motivation that organizations need to recognize and optimize.

Argyris's analysis of organizational behavior and human interaction in the workplace remains highly significant today. It will likely continue to guide academic and practical discussions on the subject in the future.

Moreover, Argyris's successful consulting career is another sign of the wide practical implications of his work in the business world beyond academia.

Summary

Chris Argyris's "The Individual and Organization" introduced a model of individual professional behavior based on the goal of achieving self-actualization. His micro-level analysis of experiential learning was a particularly original way of exploring embedded organizational problems and serves as a great contribution to performance-oriented research.

Argyris was the first to argue that conventional management practices create a conflict between organizations and individuals that is harmful to both because it treats employees like children. His core message—that formal organizations should not do this—deserves special attention. This message was supported by an explanation of human growth processes and the psychological changes that come with the transition from infancy to adulthood. The solidity of the findings has generated intellectual discussion among theorists and social scientists on the relationship between organizations and individuals.

The creation of adjustment strategies to improve relationships between organizations and individuals requires that they be viewed from different standpoints. This is an interesting academic endeavor that requires comprehensive awareness of organizational norms and group dynamics. Argyris's educational background in psychology, economics, and organizational behavior allowed him to examine and enrich behavioral science research. He did so by grasping the need for further improvements to the inharmonious relationships between individuals and organizations.

In his work, Argyris proposed that organizations should establish a flatter organizational system to facilitate data exchange to all levels. This improved organizational structure would enrich the scope of information by including the opinions and experiences of individual employees. This, he argued, would improve decision-making and foster a more harmonious and stable workplace environment.

Argyris's micro-level analysis reveals his attempt to achieve the generalization and replicability that support a successful theory. In addition, the practical nature of the work is demonstrated by the fact that organizations started to play an important role in the maturation of individual workers. They have now become increasingly regarded as a context for the realization of individual career and development objectives.

Chris Argyris's lifetime spanned a crucial period during which formal organizations gained a stronger influence over society. The nature of social and cultural evolution suggests that the relevance of his findings, ideas, and contributions will only increase in the future.

GLOSSARY

GLOSSARY OF TERMS

Adjustment strategies: how companies adjust their characteristics, operations, and products to account for differences in customers and situations. The intentional decision to alter any element of the organization is known as an adjustment strategy.

Behavioral school of management/Behaviorism: a school of thought that believes psychology should study observable behavior rather than speculate about it.

Capitalist: a person who uses their wealth to invest in trade and industry for profit in accordance with the principles of capitalism.

Chain of Command: a system in a military or civil organization by which instructions are passed from one person to another.

Classical management theorists: scholars who share the view that worker conformity and financial incentives are an efficient way to stimulate productivity.

Classical organization theory: the study for the improvement of organizations, their management systems, and their efficiencies. Developed by Frederick Taylor, the classical theory of management advocates a scientific study of tasks and workers to increase worker productivity.

Complex organizations: organizations that encompass multiple units and levels of management, and involve varied operational practices.

Double-loop learning: a concept that involves the modification of goals or decision-making rules in the light of experience. The first loop uses the goals or decision-making rules, the second loop allows their modification based on the first experience, hence "double-loop." It was created by Chris Argyris in the mid-1980s, and developed over the next decade into an effective tool.

Experiential learning: the philosophy of deriving meaning from "doing."

Extrinsic motivation: motivation that results from external influence, force, or rewards.

Flat organizational system: an organizational structure with few or no managerial levels and the easy exchange of information in all directions.

Humanism/Humanistic principles: the belief that every individual has the desire to realize his or her full potential.

Humanistic value camp/Humanistic school of thought: a group of people who believe in humanism. Humanism is the belief that every individual has the desire to realize his or her full potential.

Industrial revolution (1750–1850): a period of change and industrialization in Britain. It is linked to increased economic growth and the rapid development of industry brought about by the introduction of machinery. It was characterized by the use of steam power, the growth of factories, and the mass production of manufactured goods.

Intrinsic motivation: self-motivation based on one's own beliefs and orientation.

Learning individuals: a view that people enhance their capacities over time to create higher results or efficiencies. An individual's propensity to learn can be an important asset for their employer.

Learning organizations: a concept suggesting that organizational learning occurs when an organization supports the learning of employees and transforms itself accordingly.

Micro-level analysis: analysis that focuses on individuals in order to study their reactions, behaviors, or perspectives regarding a particular phenomenon.

Organizational action: creating and sustaining an organizational learning environment within an organization.

Organizational behavior: the study of how people interact within groups.

Organizational learning: occurs when an organization supports the learning of employees and transforms itself accordingly.

Organizational management school of thought: a group of scholars who study for the improvement of organizations, their management systems, and efficiencies.

Organizational studies: studies that apply organizational behavior theories to create more efficient business organizations.

Performance-oriented research: research that studies factors influencing the output of the company for the purpose of maximizing outputs and diminishing inefficiencies.

Psychoanalysis: a system of psychological theory and therapy which aims to treat mental disorders by investigating the interaction of conscious and unconscious elements in the mind. It brings repressed fears and conflicts into the conscious mind with techniques such as dream interpretation and free association.

Pyramidal scheme/Pyramidal value system: a top-down management approach in which decision-making flows from top managers down to bottom levels.

Scientific management theory: also known as Taylorism, a theory that studies workflows and how economic efficiency can be achieved.

Self-actualization: the state of realizing, or the perpetual human attempt to realize, one's full potential.

Signal Corps: a branch of the United States military which develops, tests, and manages communication and information systems for the armed forces.

Single-loop learning: the repeated attempt to solve an ongoing problem with the same tool(s).

Skilled Incompetence: a condition in which people excel at doing what they shouldn't because it seems right. For example, managers are "skilled" because they act without thinking. They are "incompetent" because their skill produces unintended results.

Span of Control: the area of activity and number of functions, people, or things for which an individual or organization is responsible.

Strategy Adaptation Capabilities: the power or ability to adapt or alter the current strategy of an organization.

Task Specialization: the process of focusing one's occupational concentration on a specific area of expertise.

Theory X: a theory on human motivation stating that employees dislike and try to avoid work. Theory X suggests an authoritarian management style.

Theory Y: a theory on human motivation suggesting that employees will be committed to their work and will exercise self-control to achieve organizational goals. Theory Y promotes a participative style of management. It was developed by Douglas McGregor in his 1960 book *The Human Side of Enterprise*.

Theory Z: a theory on human motivation suggesting that increasing employee loyalty to the company is possible by providing a lifelong job that has a strong focus on the well-being of the employee.

World War II: a global war that lasted from 1939 to 1945 between the Allied and Axis Forces.

PEOPLE MENTIONED IN THE TEXT

Mark Dodgson (b. 1957) is an Australian academic and author. His research on the innovation process has influenced innovation management and policy worldwide.

Peter Drucker (1909–2005) was an Austrian-born American management consultant, educator, and author whose writings contributed to the philosophical and practical foundations of the modern business corporation.

Marlena Fiol is a professor of management at University of Colorado Denver.

Mary Parker Follett (1868–1933) was an American social worker, management consultant, and philosopher. She is known as a major contributor to the fields of organizational theory and behavior.

Sigmund Freud (1856–1939) was an Austrian neurologist. He is known as the founding father of psychoanalysis—a clinical method for treating psychopathology through dialogue between a patient and a psychoanalyst.

Robert M. Fulmer is a specialist in strategic leadership development and an academic director for Duke Corporate Education. He is Professor Emeritus at the College of William & Mary.

Lillian Gilbreth (1878–1972) was an American psychologist and industrial engineer. She was one of the first working female engineers to hold a Ph.D. She is held to be the first true industrial/organizational psychologist.

George P. Huber (b. 1936) is the Chair Emeritus in Business Administration at the University of Texas, Austin. He is a Fellow of the Academy of Management and of the Decision Sciences Institute.

Kurt Lewin (1890–1947) was a German American psychologist known as one of the modern pioneers of social, organizational, and applied psychology in the United States. He was a distinguished contributor to social and organizational psychology.

Niklas Luhmann (1927–1998) was a German sociologist. He is recognized as one of the most important social theorists of the twentieth century due to his contribution to systems theory.

Abraham Maslow (1908–1970) was an American psychologist and is known for creating Maslow's hierarchy of needs.

Elton Mayo (1880–1949) was an Australian psychologist and professor of industrial studies. He is known as an active contributor to management theory.

Douglas McGregor (1906–1964) was a management professor at the MIT Sloan School of Management. He is known for developing Theories X and Y.

Delbert C. Miller (1913–1998) was an American organizational theorist and Professor of sociology and business administration at Indiana University, Bloomington. He is noted for his work on industrial sociology.

Ikujiro Nonaka (b. 1935) is a Japanese organizational theorist, best known for his study of knowledge management.

Robert Putnam (b. 1941) is an American political scientist. He is the Peter and Isabel Malkin Professor of Public Policy at the Harvard University John F. Kennedy School of Government.

Edgar Schein (b. 1928) is a former professor at the MIT Sloan School of Management. He is widely known for his contribution to organizational development.

Donald Schön (1930–1997) was a philosopher and professor in urban planning at the Massachusetts Institute of Technology. He developed the concept of reflective practice and contributed to the theory of organizational learning.

Peter Senge (b. 1947) is an American scientist and director of the Center for Organizational Learning at the MIT Sloan School of Management. He is the founder of the Society for Organizational Learning.

Diana McLain Smith is the chief executive partner of New Profit Inc., a national venture philanthropy firm. She is a former partner at the Monitor Group.

Hirotaka Takeuchi (b. 1946) is a Japanese organizational theorist best known for his study of knowledge management.

William Whyte (1914–2000) was a sociologist predominantly known for his ethnographic study in urban sociology. A pioneer in participant observation, he lived for four years in an Italian community in Boston to research social relations of street gangs in Boston's North End.

WORKS CITED

WORKS CITED

Anderson, Jill. "Remembering Professor Chris Argyris." *Harvard School of Education News and Events*. November 22, 2013. Accessed January 22, 2018. https://www.gse.harvard.edu/news/13/11/remembering-professor-chris-argyris.

Argyris, Chris. "Creating Effective Research Relationships in an Organization." *Human Organization* 17 (1958): 34–40.

"The Individual and Organization: An Empirical Test." *Administrative Science Quarterly* 4 (1959): 146–67.

"The Individual and Organization: Some Problems of Mutual Adjustment." *Administrative Science Quarterly* 2 (1957): 1–24.

Integrating the Individual and the Organization. New York: Routledge, 2017.

"Management Implications of Recent Social Science Research." *Personnel Administration* 21 (1958): 5–10.

"The Organization: What Makes It Healthy?" *Harvard Business Review* 36 (1958): 107–16.

Argyris, Chris, and Donald A. Schön. *Organizational Learning: A Theory of Action Perspective*, Reading, Mass: Addison Wesley, 1978.

Theory in Practice: Increasing Professional Effectiveness. San Francisco: Jossey-Bass, 1974.

Argyris, Chris, Robert Putnam, and Diana McLain Smith. *Action Science*. San Francisco: Jossey-Bass, 1985.

Dodgson, M., 1993. "Organizational learning: a review of some literatures." *Organization studies*, 14(3) (1993): 375-394.

Fiol, C.M. and Lyles, M.A., "Organizational learning." *Academy of Management Review*, 10(4) (1985): 803-813.

Fulmer, Robert M., and Bernard J. Keys. "A Conversation with Chris Argyris: The Father of Organizational Learning." *Organizational Dynamics*, 27(2) (1998): 21–32.

Hatch, Mary Jo, and Ann L. Cunliffe. *Organization Theory*. Oxford: Oxford University Press, 2013.

Huber, G.P., 1991. "Organizational learning: The contributing processes and the literatures." *Organization Science*, 2(1): 88-115.

Luhmann, Niklas. *Ecological Communication.* Cambridge: Polity Press, 1989.

Maslow, Abraham H. *The Farther Reaches of Human Nature.* New York: Viking Press, 1971.

"A Theory of Human Motivation." *Psychological Review* 50 (1943): 360–96.

McGregor, Douglas. *The Human Side of Enterprise.* McGraw-Hill Professional, 2006.

Putnam, Robert. "A Biography of Chris Argyris." *Journal of Applied Behavioral Science* 31 (1995): 253–5.

Ramage, Magnus, and Karen Shipp. *Systems Thinkers*. London: Springer, 2009.

Senge, Peter. *The Fifth Discipline: The Art and Practice of the Learning Organization.* London: Random House, 1990.

THE MACAT LIBRARY
BY DISCIPLINE

The Macat Library By Discipline

AFRICANA STUDIES

Chinua Achebe's *An Image of Africa: Racism in Conrad's Heart of Darkness*
W. E. B. Du Bois's *The Souls of Black Folk*
Zora Neale Huston's *Characteristics of Negro Expression*
Martin Luther King Jr's *Why We Can't Wait*
Toni Morrison's *Playing in the Dark: Whiteness in the American Literary Imagination*

ANTHROPOLOGY

Arjun Appadurai's *Modernity at Large: Cultural Dimensions of Globalisation*
Philippe Ariès's *Centuries of Childhood*
Franz Boas's *Race, Language and Culture*
Kim Chan & Renée Mauborgne's *Blue Ocean Strategy*
Jared Diamond's *Guns, Germs & Steel: the Fate of Human Societies*
Jared Diamond's *Collapse: How Societies Choose to Fail or Survive*
E. E. Evans-Pritchard's *Witchcraft, Oracles and Magic Among the Azande*
James Ferguson's *The Anti-Politics Machine*
Clifford Geertz's *The Interpretation of Cultures*
David Graeber's *Debt: the First 5000 Years*
Karen Ho's *Liquidated: An Ethnography of Wall Street*
Geert Hofstede's *Culture's Consequences: Comparing Values, Behaviors, Institutes and Organizations across Nations*
Claude Lévi-Strauss's *Structural Anthropology*
Jay Macleod's *Ain't No Makin' It: Aspirations and Attainment in a Low-Income Neighborhood*
Saba Mahmood's *The Politics of Piety: The Islamic Revival and the Feminist Subject*
Marcel Mauss's *The Gift*

BUSINESS

Jean Lave & Etienne Wenger's *Situated Learning*
Theodore Levitt's *Marketing Myopia*
Burton G. Malkiel's *A Random Walk Down Wall Street*
Douglas McGregor's *The Human Side of Enterprise*
Michael Porter's *Competitive Strategy: Creating and Sustaining Superior Performance*
John Kotter's *Leading Change*
C. K. Prahalad & Gary Hamel's *The Core Competence of the Corporation*

CRIMINOLOGY

Michelle Alexander's *The New Jim Crow: Mass Incarceration in the Age of Colorblindness*
Michael R. Gottfredson & Travis Hirschi's *A General Theory of Crime*
Richard Herrnstein & Charles A. Murray's *The Bell Curve: Intelligence and Class Structure in American Life*
Elizabeth Loftus's *Eyewitness Testimony*
Jay Macleod's *Ain't No Makin' It: Aspirations and Attainment in a Low-Income Neighborhood*
Philip Zimbardo's *The Lucifer Effect*

ECONOMICS

Janet Abu-Lughod's *Before European Hegemony*
Ha-Joon Chang's *Kicking Away the Ladder*
David Brion Davis's *The Problem of Slavery in the Age of Revolution*
Milton Friedman's *The Role of Monetary Policy*
Milton Friedman's *Capitalism and Freedom*
David Graeber's *Debt: the First 5000 Years*
Friedrich Hayek's *The Road to Serfdom*
Karen Ho's *Liquidated: An Ethnography of Wall Street*

John Maynard Keynes's *The General Theory of Employment, Interest and Money*
Charles P. Kindleberger's *Manias, Panics and Crashes*
Robert Lucas's *Why Doesn't Capital Flow from Rich to Poor Countries?*
Burton G. Malkiel's *A Random Walk Down Wall Street*
Thomas Robert Malthus's *An Essay on the Principle of Population*
Karl Marx's *Capital*
Thomas Piketty's *Capital in the Twenty-First Century*
Amartya Sen's *Development as Freedom*
Adam Smith's *The Wealth of Nations*
Nassim Nicholas Taleb's *The Black Swan: The Impact of the Highly Improbable*
Amos Tversky's & Daniel Kahneman's *Judgment under Uncertainty: Heuristics and Biases*
Mahbub Ul Haq's *Reflections on Human Development*
Max Weber's *The Protestant Ethic and the Spirit of Capitalism*

FEMINISM AND GENDER STUDIES

Judith Butler's *Gender Trouble*
Simone De Beauvoir's *The Second Sex*
Michel Foucault's *History of Sexuality*
Betty Friedan's *The Feminine Mystique*
Saba Mahmood's *The Politics of Piety: The Islamic Revival and the Feminist Subject*
Joan Wallach Scott's *Gender and the Politics of History*
Mary Wollstonecraft's *A Vindication of the Rights of Woman*
Virginia Woolf's *A Room of One's Own*

GEOGRAPHY

The Brundtland Report's *Our Common Future*
Rachel Carson's *Silent Spring*
Charles Darwin's *On the Origin of Species*
James Ferguson's *The Anti-Politics Machine*
Jane Jacobs's *The Death and Life of Great American Cities*
James Lovelock's *Gaia: A New Look at Life on Earth*
Amartya Sen's *Development as Freedom*
Mathis Wackernagel & William Rees's *Our Ecological Footprint*

HISTORY

Janet Abu-Lughod's *Before European Hegemony*
Benedict Anderson's *Imagined Communities*
Bernard Bailyn's *The Ideological Origins of the American Revolution*
Hanna Batatu's *The Old Social Classes And The Revolutionary Movements Of Iraq*
Christopher Browning's *Ordinary Men: Reserve Police Batallion 101 and the Final Solution in Poland*
Edmund Burke's *Reflections on the Revolution in France*
William Cronon's *Nature's Metropolis: Chicago And The Great West*
Alfred W. Crosby's *The Columbian Exchange*
Hamid Dabashi's *Iran: A People Interrupted*
David Brion Davis's *The Problem of Slavery in the Age of Revolution*
Nathalie Zemon Davis's *The Return of Martin Guerre*
Jared Diamond's *Guns, Germs & Steel: the Fate of Human Societies*
Frank Dikotter's *Mao's Great Famine*
John W Dower's *War Without Mercy: Race And Power In The Pacific War*
W. E. B. Du Bois's *The Souls of Black Folk*
Richard J. Evans's *In Defence of History*
Lucien Febvre's *The Problem of Unbelief in the 16th Century*
Sheila Fitzpatrick's *Everyday Stalinism*

The Macat Library By Discipline

Eric Foner's *Reconstruction: America's Unfinished Revolution, 1863-1877*
Michel Foucault's *Discipline and Punish*
Michel Foucault's *History of Sexuality*
Francis Fukuyama's *The End of History and the Last Man*
John Lewis Gaddis's *We Now Know: Rethinking Cold War History*
Ernest Gellner's *Nations and Nationalism*
Eugene Genovese's *Roll, Jordan, Roll: The World the Slaves Made*
Carlo Ginzburg's *The Night Battles*
Daniel Goldhagen's *Hitler's Willing Executioners*
Jack Goldstone's *Revolution and Rebellion in the Early Modern World*
Antonio Gramsci's *The Prison Notebooks*
Alexander Hamilton, John Jay & James Madison's *The Federalist Papers*
Christopher Hill's *The World Turned Upside Down*
Carole Hillenbrand's *The Crusades: Islamic Perspectives*
Thomas Hobbes's *Leviathan*
Eric Hobsbawm's *The Age Of Revolution*
John A. Hobson's *Imperialism: A Study*
Albert Hourani's *History of the Arab Peoples*
Samuel P. Huntington's *The Clash of Civilizations and the Remaking of World Order*
C. L. R. James's *The Black Jacobins*
Tony Judt's *Postwar: A History of Europe Since 1945*
Ernst Kantorowicz's *The King's Two Bodies: A Study in Medieval Political Theology*
Paul Kennedy's *The Rise and Fall of the Great Powers*
Ian Kershaw's *The "Hitler Myth": Image and Reality in the Third Reich*
John Maynard Keynes's *The General Theory of Employment, Interest and Money*
Charles P. Kindleberger's *Manias, Panics and Crashes*
Martin Luther King Jr's *Why We Can't Wait*
Henry Kissinger's *World Order: Reflections on the Character of Nations and the Course of History*
Thomas Kuhn's *The Structure of Scientific Revolutions*
Georges Lefebvre's *The Coming of the French Revolution*
John Locke's *Two Treatises of Government*
Niccolò Machiavelli's *The Prince*
Thomas Robert Malthus's *An Essay on the Principle of Population*
Mahmood Mamdani's *Citizen and Subject: Contemporary Africa And The Legacy Of Late Colonialism*
Karl Marx's *Capital*
Stanley Milgram's *Obedience to Authority*
John Stuart Mill's *On Liberty*
Thomas Paine's *Common Sense*
Thomas Paine's *Rights of Man*
Geoffrey Parker's *Global Crisis: War, Climate Change and Catastrophe in the Seventeenth Century*
Jonathan Riley-Smith's *The First Crusade and the Idea of Crusading*
Jean-Jacques Rousseau's *The Social Contract*
Joan Wallach Scott's *Gender and the Politics of History*
Theda Skocpol's *States and Social Revolutions*
Adam Smith's *The Wealth of Nations*
Timothy Snyder's *Bloodlands: Europe Between Hitler and Stalin*
Sun Tzu's *The Art of War*
Keith Thomas's *Religion and the Decline of Magic*
Thucydides's *The History of the Peloponnesian War*
Frederick Jackson Turner's *The Significance of the Frontier in American History*
Odd Arne Westad's *The Global Cold War: Third World Interventions And The Making Of Our Times*

LITERATURE

Chinua Achebe's *An Image of Africa: Racism in Conrad's Heart of Darkness*
Roland Barthes's *Mythologies*
Homi K. Bhabha's *The Location of Culture*
Judith Butler's *Gender Trouble*
Simone De Beauvoir's *The Second Sex*
Ferdinand De Saussure's *Course in General Linguistics*
T. S. Eliot's *The Sacred Wood: Essays on Poetry and Criticism*
Zora Neale Huston's *Characteristics of Negro Expression*
Toni Morrison's *Playing in the Dark: Whiteness in the American Literary Imagination*
Edward Said's *Orientalism*
Gayatri Chakravorty Spivak's *Can the Subaltern Speak?*
Mary Wollstonecraft's *A Vindication of the Rights of Women*
Virginia Woolf's *A Room of One's Own*

PHILOSOPHY

Elizabeth Anscombe's *Modern Moral Philosophy*
Hannah Arendt's *The Human Condition*
Aristotle's *Metaphysics*
Aristotle's *Nicomachean Ethics*
Edmund Gettier's *Is Justified True Belief Knowledge?*
Georg Wilhelm Friedrich Hegel's *Phenomenology of Spirit*
David Hume's *Dialogues Concerning Natural Religion*
David Hume's *The Enquiry for Human Understanding*
Immanuel Kant's *Religion within the Boundaries of Mere Reason*
Immanuel Kant's *Critique of Pure Reason*
Søren Kierkegaard's *The Sickness Unto Death*
Søren Kierkegaard's *Fear and Trembling*
C. S. Lewis's *The Abolition of Man*
Alasdair MacIntyre's *After Virtue*
Marcus Aurelius's *Meditations*
Friedrich Nietzsche's *On the Genealogy of Morality*
Friedrich Nietzsche's *Beyond Good and Evil*
Plato's *Republic*
Plato's *Symposium*
Jean-Jacques Rousseau's *The Social Contract*
Gilbert Ryle's *The Concept of Mind*
Baruch Spinoza's *Ethics*
Sun Tzu's *The Art of War*
Ludwig Wittgenstein's *Philosophical Investigations*

POLITICS

Benedict Anderson's *Imagined Communities*
Aristotle's *Politics*
Bernard Bailyn's *The Ideological Origins of the American Revolution*
Edmund Burke's *Reflections on the Revolution in France*
John C. Calhoun's *A Disquisition on Government*
Ha-Joon Chang's *Kicking Away the Ladder*
Hamid Dabashi's *Iran: A People Interrupted*
Hamid Dabashi's *Theology of Discontent: The Ideological Foundation of the Islamic Revolution in Iran*
Robert Dahl's *Democracy and its Critics*
Robert Dahl's *Who Governs?*
David Brion Davis's *The Problem of Slavery in the Age of Revolution*

The Macat Library By Discipline

Alexis De Tocqueville's *Democracy in America*
James Ferguson's *The Anti-Politics Machine*
Frank Dikotter's *Mao's Great Famine*
Sheila Fitzpatrick's *Everyday Stalinism*
Eric Foner's *Reconstruction: America's Unfinished Revolution, 1863-1877*
Milton Friedman's *Capitalism and Freedom*
Francis Fukuyama's *The End of History and the Last Man*
John Lewis Gaddis's *We Now Know: Rethinking Cold War History*
Ernest Gellner's *Nations and Nationalism*
David Graeber's *Debt: the First 5000 Years*
Antonio Gramsci's *The Prison Notebooks*
Alexander Hamilton, John Jay & James Madison's *The Federalist Papers*
Friedrich Hayek's *The Road to Serfdom*
Christopher Hill's *The World Turned Upside Down*
Thomas Hobbes's *Leviathan*
John A. Hobson's *Imperialism: A Study*
Samuel P. Huntington's *The Clash of Civilizations and the Remaking of World Order*
Tony Judt's *Postwar: A History of Europe Since 1945*
David C. Kang's *China Rising: Peace, Power and Order in East Asia*
Paul Kennedy's *The Rise and Fall of Great Powers*
Robert Keohane's *After Hegemony*
Martin Luther King Jr.'s *Why We Can't Wait*
Henry Kissinger's *World Order: Reflections on the Character of Nations and the Course of History*
John Locke's *Two Treatises of Government*
Niccolò Machiavelli's *The Prince*
Thomas Robert Malthus's *An Essay on the Principle of Population*
Mahmood Mamdani's *Citizen and Subject: Contemporary Africa And The Legacy Of Late Colonialism*
Karl Marx's *Capital*
John Stuart Mill's *On Liberty*
John Stuart Mill's *Utilitarianism*
Hans Morgenthau's *Politics Among Nations*
Thomas Paine's *Common Sense*
Thomas Paine's *Rights of Man*
Thomas Piketty's *Capital in the Twenty-First Century*
Robert D. Putman's *Bowling Alone*
John Rawls's *Theory of Justice*
Jean-Jacques Rousseau's *The Social Contract*
Theda Skocpol's *States and Social Revolutions*
Adam Smith's *The Wealth of Nations*
Sun Tzu's *The Art of War*
Henry David Thoreau's *Civil Disobedience*
Thucydides's *The History of the Peloponnesian War*
Kenneth Waltz's *Theory of International Politics*
Max Weber's *Politics as a Vocation*
Odd Arne Westad's *The Global Cold War: Third World Interventions And The Making Of Our Times*

POSTCOLONIAL STUDIES

Roland Barthes's *Mythologies*
Frantz Fanon's *Black Skin, White Masks*
Homi K. Bhabha's *The Location of Culture*
Gustavo Gutiérrez's *A Theology of Liberation*
Edward Said's *Orientalism*
Gayatri Chakravorty Spivak's *Can the Subaltern Speak?*

PSYCHOLOGY

Gordon Allport's *The Nature of Prejudice*
Alan Baddeley & Graham Hitch's *Aggression: A Social Learning Analysis*
Albert Bandura's *Aggression: A Social Learning Analysis*
Leon Festinger's *A Theory of Cognitive Dissonance*
Sigmund Freud's *The Interpretation of Dreams*
Betty Friedan's *The Feminine Mystique*
Michael R. Gottfredson & Travis Hirschi's *A General Theory of Crime*
Eric Hoffer's *The True Believer: Thoughts on the Nature of Mass Movements*
William James's *Principles of Psychology*
Elizabeth Loftus's *Eyewitness Testimony*
A. H. Maslow's *A Theory of Human Motivation*
Stanley Milgram's *Obedience to Authority*
Steven Pinker's *The Better Angels of Our Nature*
Oliver Sacks's *The Man Who Mistook His Wife For a Hat*
Richard Thaler & Cass Sunstein's *Nudge: Improving Decisions About Health, Wealth and Happiness*
Amos Tversky's *Judgment under Uncertainty: Heuristics and Biases*
Philip Zimbardo's *The Lucifer Effect*

SCIENCE

Rachel Carson's *Silent Spring*
William Cronon's *Nature's Metropolis: Chicago And The Great West*
Alfred W. Crosby's *The Columbian Exchange*
Charles Darwin's *On the Origin of Species*
Richard Dawkin's *The Selfish Gene*
Thomas Kuhn's *The Structure of Scientific Revolutions*
Geoffrey Parker's *Global Crisis: War, Climate Change and Catastrophe in the Seventeenth Century*
Mathis Wackernagel & William Rees's *Our Ecological Footprint*

SOCIOLOGY

Michelle Alexander's *The New Jim Crow: Mass Incarceration in the Age of Colorblindness*
Gordon Allport's *The Nature of Prejudice*
Albert Bandura's *Aggression: A Social Learning Analysis*
Hanna Batatu's *The Old Social Classes And The Revolutionary Movements Of Iraq*
Ha-Joon Chang's *Kicking Away the Ladder*
W. E. B. Du Bois's *The Souls of Black Folk*
Émile Durkheim's *On Suicide*
Frantz Fanon's *Black Skin, White Masks*
Frantz Fanon's *The Wretched of the Earth*
Eric Foner's *Reconstruction: America's Unfinished Revolution, 1863-1877*
Eugene Genovese's *Roll, Jordan, Roll: The World the Slaves Made*
Jack Goldstone's *Revolution and Rebellion in the Early Modern World*
Antonio Gramsci's *The Prison Notebooks*
Richard Herrnstein & Charles A Murray's *The Bell Curve: Intelligence and Class Structure in American Life*
Eric Hoffer's *The True Believer: Thoughts on the Nature of Mass Movements*
Jane Jacobs's *The Death and Life of Great American Cities*
Robert Lucas's *Why Doesn't Capital Flow from Rich to Poor Countries?*
Jay Macleod's *Ain't No Makin' It: Aspirations and Attainment in a Low Income Neighborhood*
Elaine May's *Homeward Bound: American Families in the Cold War Era*
Douglas McGregor's *The Human Side of Enterprise*
C. Wright Mills's *The Sociological Imagination*

The Macat Library By Discipline

Thomas Piketty's *Capital in the Twenty-First Century*
Robert D. Putman's *Bowling Alone*
David Riesman's *The Lonely Crowd: A Study of the Changing American Character*
Edward Said's *Orientalism*
Joan Wallach Scott's *Gender and the Politics of History*
Theda Skocpol's *States and Social Revolutions*
Max Weber's *The Protestant Ethic and the Spirit of Capitalism*

THEOLOGY

Augustine's *Confessions*
Benedict's *Rule of St Benedict*
Gustavo Gutiérrez's *A Theology of Liberation*
Carole Hillenbrand's *The Crusades: Islamic Perspectives*
David Hume's *Dialogues Concerning Natural Religion*
Immanuel Kant's *Religion within the Boundaries of Mere Reason*
Ernst Kantorowicz's *The King's Two Bodies: A Study in Medieval Political Theology*
Søren Kierkegaard's *The Sickness Unto Death*
C. S. Lewis's *The Abolition of Man*
Saba Mahmood's *The Politics of Piety: The Islamic Revival and the Feminist Subject*
Baruch Spinoza's *Ethics*
Keith Thomas's *Religion and the Decline of Magic*

COMING SOON

Chris Argyris's *The Individual and the Organisation*
Seyla Benhabib's *The Rights of Others*
Walter Benjamin's *The Work Of Art in the Age of Mechanical Reproduction*
John Berger's *Ways of Seeing*
Pierre Bourdieu's *Outline of a Theory of Practice*
Mary Douglas's *Purity and Danger*
Roland Dworkin's *Taking Rights Seriously*
James G. March's *Exploration and Exploitation in Organisational Learning*
Ikujiro Nonaka's *A Dynamic Theory of Organizational Knowledge Creation*
Griselda Pollock's *Vision and Difference*
Amartya Sen's *Inequality Re-Examined*
Susan Sontag's *On Photography*
Yasser Tabbaa's *The Transformation of Islamic Art*
Ludwig von Mises's *Theory of Money and Credit*

Macat Disciplines
Access the greatest ideas and thinkers across entire disciplines, including

Postcolonial Studies

Roland Barthes's *Mythologies*
Frantz Fanon's *Black Skin, White Masks*
Homi K. Bhabha's *The Location of Culture*
Gustavo Gutiérrez's *A Theology of Liberation*
Edward Said's *Orientalism*
Gayatri Chakravorty Spivak's *Can the Subaltern Speak?*

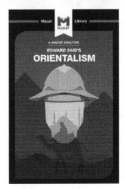

Macat analyses are available from all good bookshops and libraries.

Access hundreds of analyses through one, multimedia tool.

Join free for one month **library.macat.com**

Macat Disciplines

Access the greatest ideas and thinkers across entire disciplines, including

AFRICANA STUDIES

Chinua Achebe's *An Image of Africa: Racism in Conrad's Heart of Darkness*

W. E. B. Du Bois's *The Souls of Black Folk*

Zora Neale Hurston's *Characteristics of Negro Expression*

Martin Luther King Jr.'s *Why We Can't Wait*

Toni Morrison's *Playing in the Dark: Whiteness in the American Literary Imagination*

Macat analyses are available from all good bookshops and libraries.

Access hundreds of analyses through one, multimedia tool.

Macat Disciplines

*Access the greatest ideas and thinkers
across entire disciplines, including*

FEMINISM, GENDER AND QUEER STUDIES

Simone De Beauvoir's
The Second Sex

Michel Foucault's
History of Sexuality

Betty Friedan's
The Feminine Mystique

Saba Mahmood's
*The Politics of Piety:
The Islamic Revival and
the Feminist Subject*

Joan Wallach Scott's
*Gender and the
Politics of History*

Mary Wollstonecraft's
*A Vindication of the
Rights of Woman*

Virginia Woolf's
A Room of One's Own

Judith Butler's
Gender Trouble

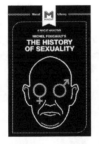

Macat analyses are available from all good bookshops and libraries.

Access hundreds of analyses through one, multimedia tool.

Join free for one month **library.macat.com**

Macat Disciplines

Access the greatest ideas and thinkers across entire disciplines, including

CRIMINOLOGY

Michelle Alexander's
The New Jim Crow: Mass Incarceration in the Age of Colorblindness

Michael R. Gottfredson & Travis Hirschi's
A General Theory of Crime

Elizabeth Loftus's
Eyewitness Testimony

Richard Herrnstein & Charles A. Murray's
The Bell Curve: Intelligence and Class Structure in American Life

Jay Macleod's
Ain't No Makin' It: Aspirations and Attainment in a Low-Income Neighborhood

Philip Zimbardo's
The Lucifer Effect

Macat analyses are available from all good bookshops and libraries.

Access hundreds of analyses through one, multimedia tool.

Macat Disciplines

*Access the greatest ideas and thinkers
across entire disciplines, including*

INEQUALITY

Ha-Joon Chang's, *Kicking Away the Ladder*

David Graeber's, *Debt: The First 5000 Years*

Robert E. Lucas's, *Why Doesn't Capital Flow from
Rich To Poor Countries?*

Thomas Piketty's, *Capital in the Twenty-First Century*

Amartya Sen's, *Inequality Re-Examined*

Mahbub Ul Haq's, *Reflections on Human Development*

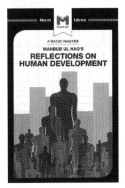

Printed in the United States
by Baker & Taylor Publisher Services